About FUCK OFF

Outstanding Swear Word To Color For Stress Releasing

Ja Millie Hawthorn

Happy Coloring!

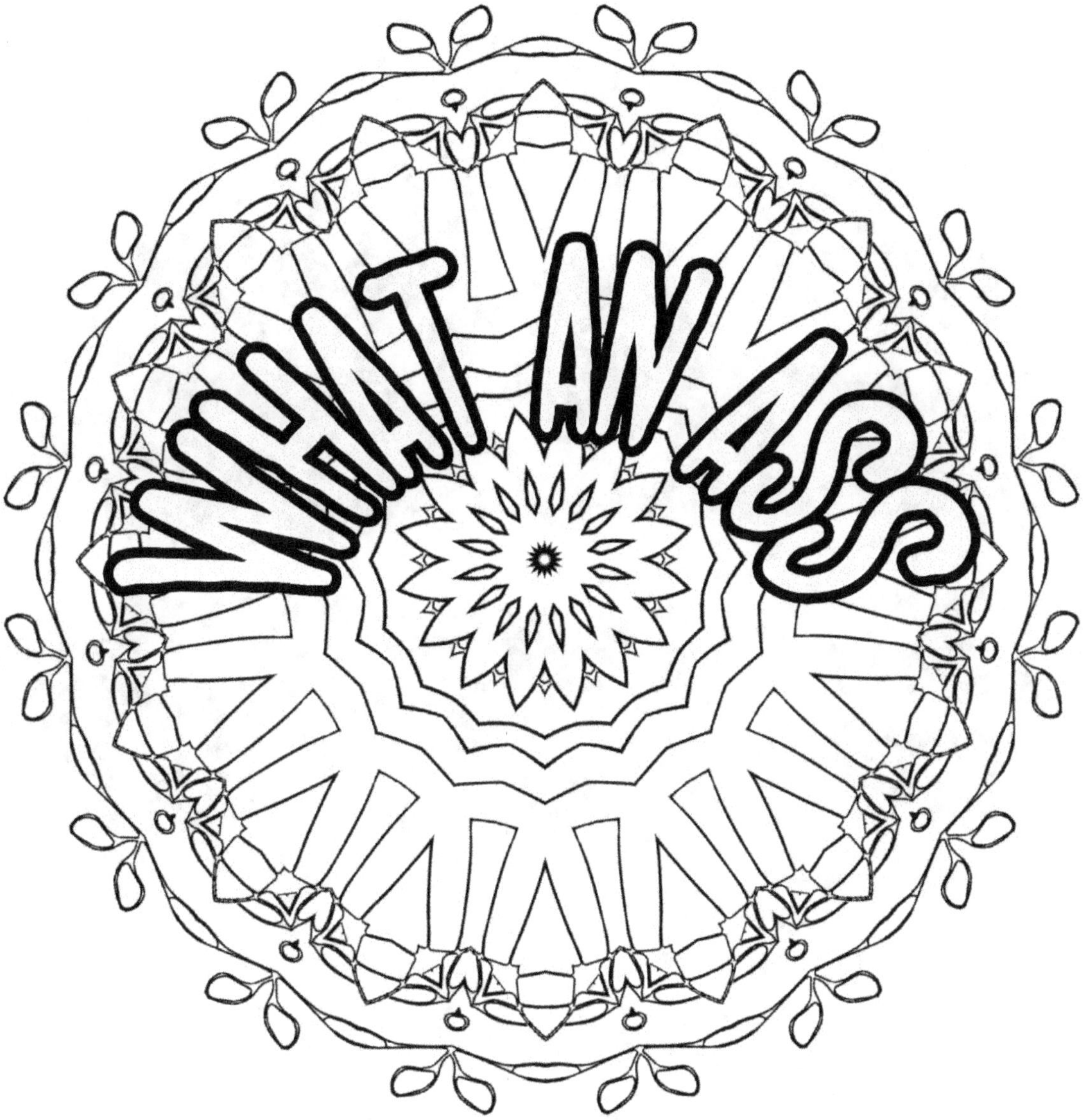
WHAT AN ASS

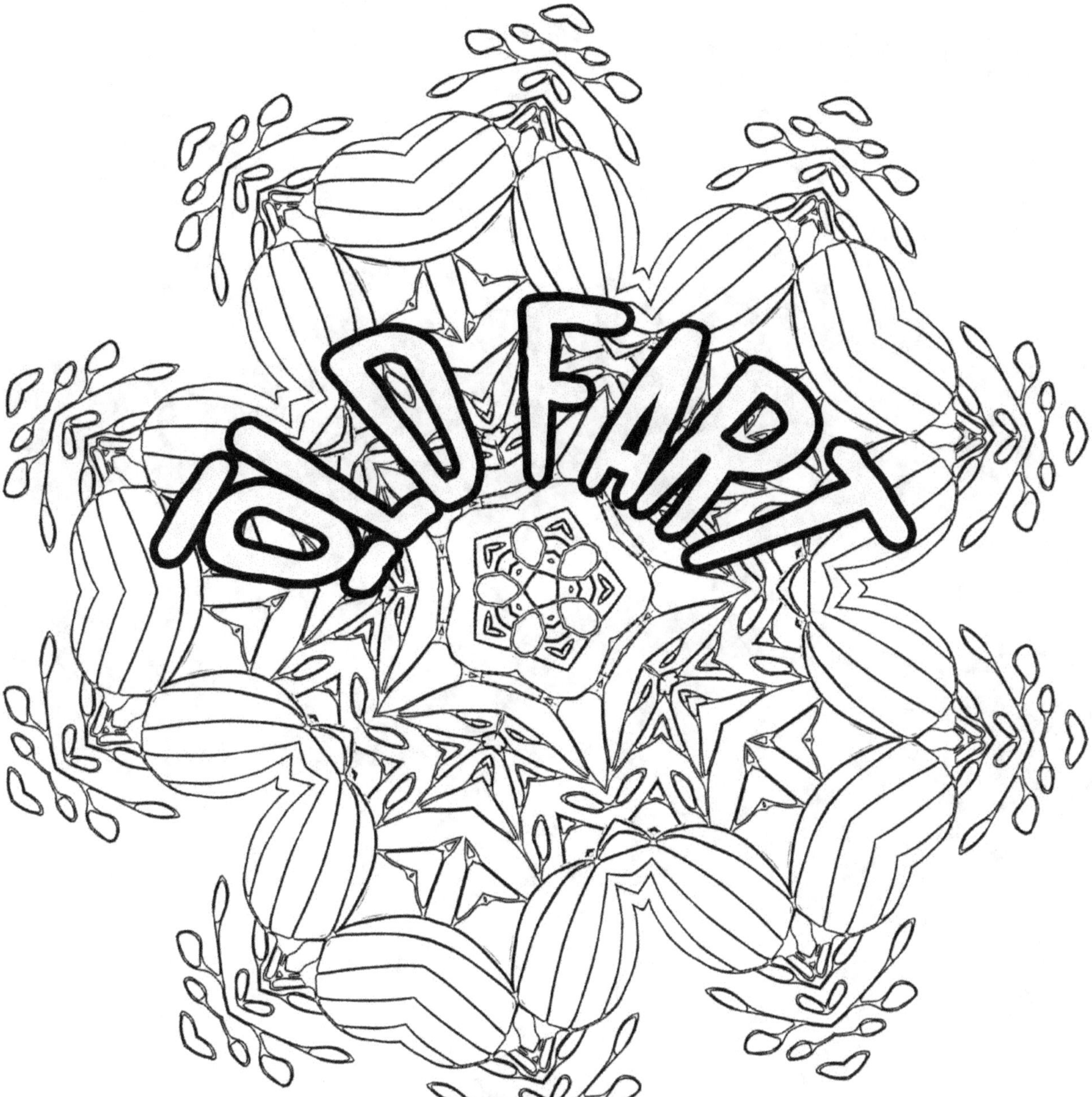
OLD FART

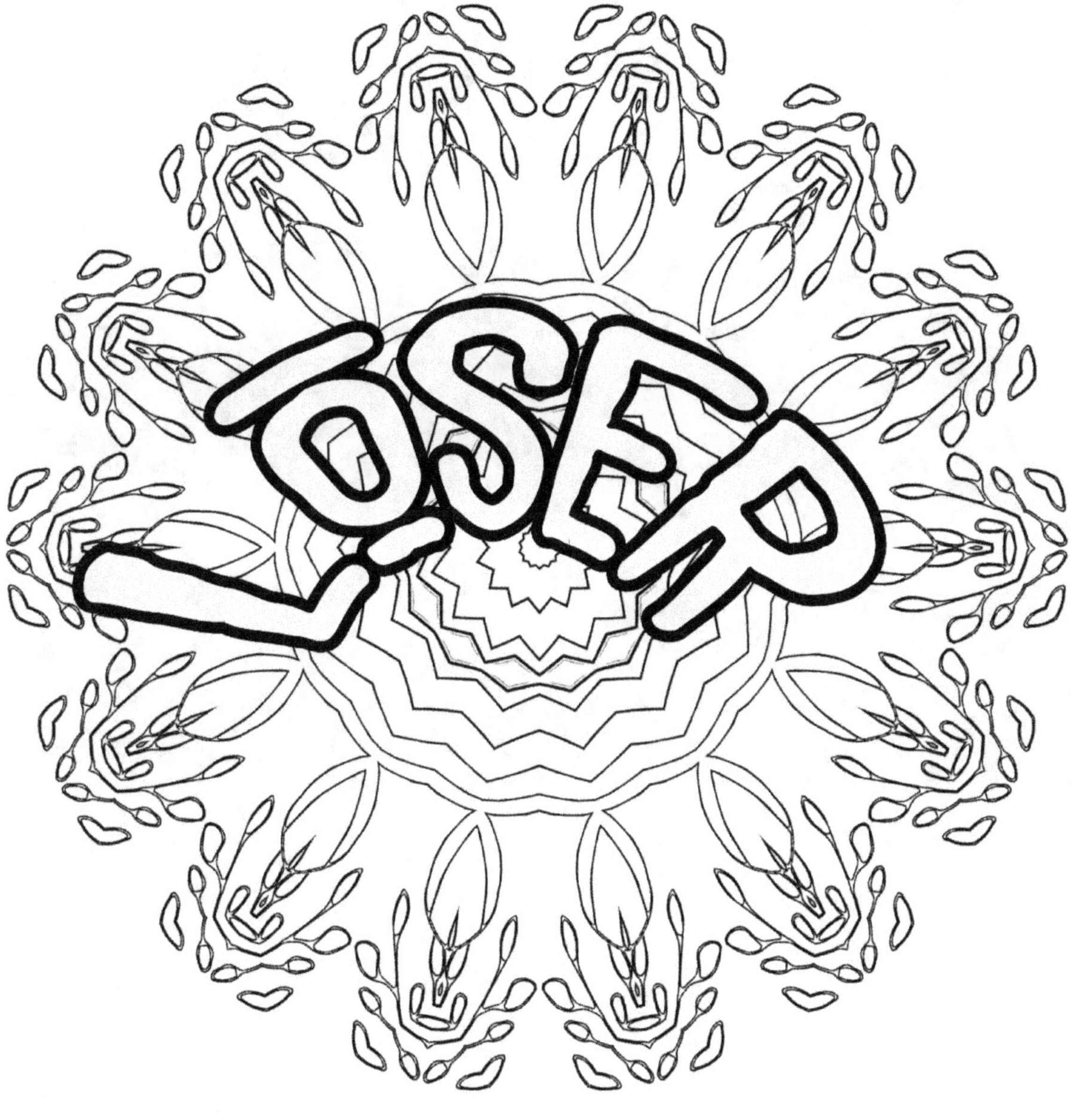
LOSER

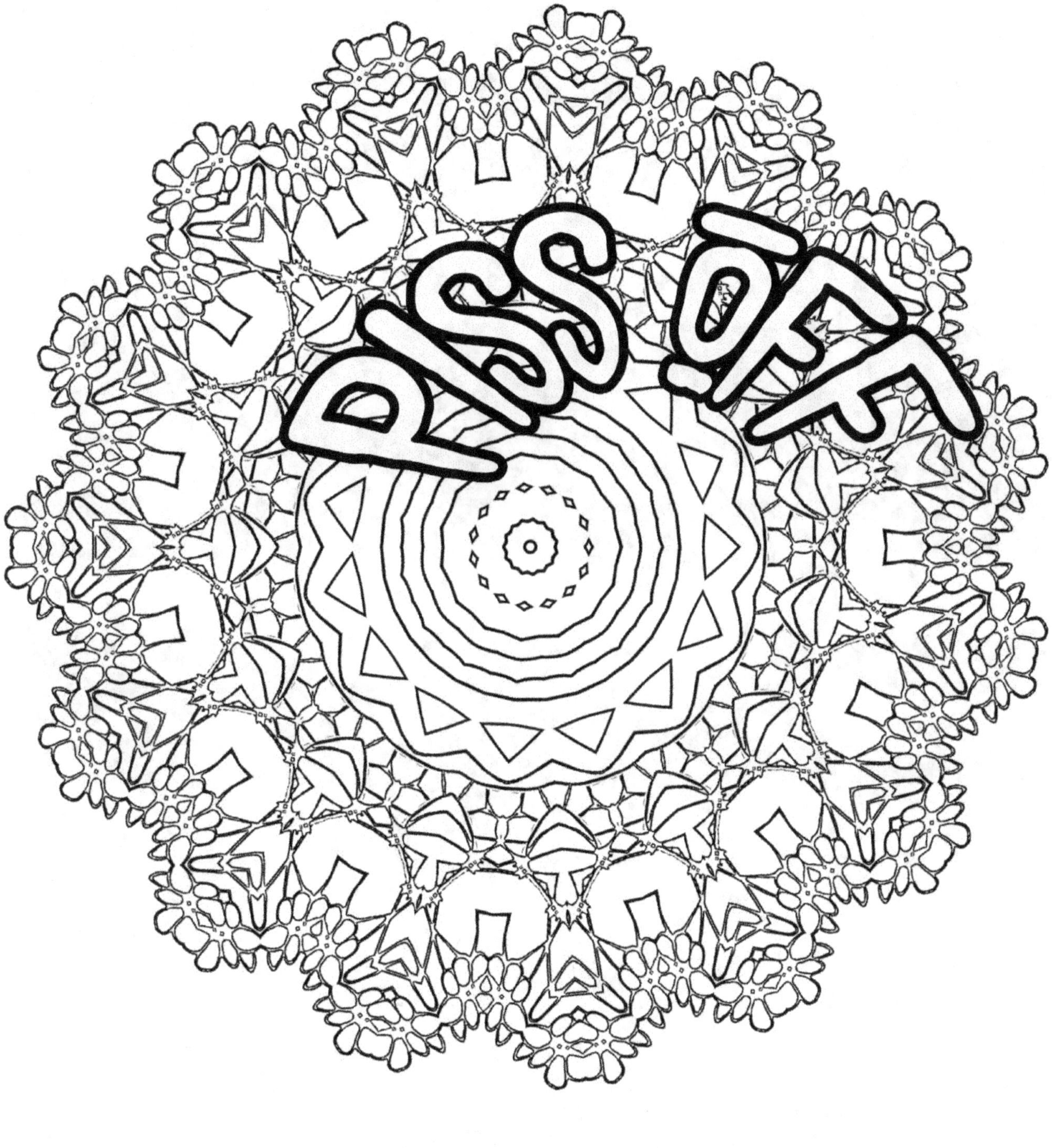
PISS OFF

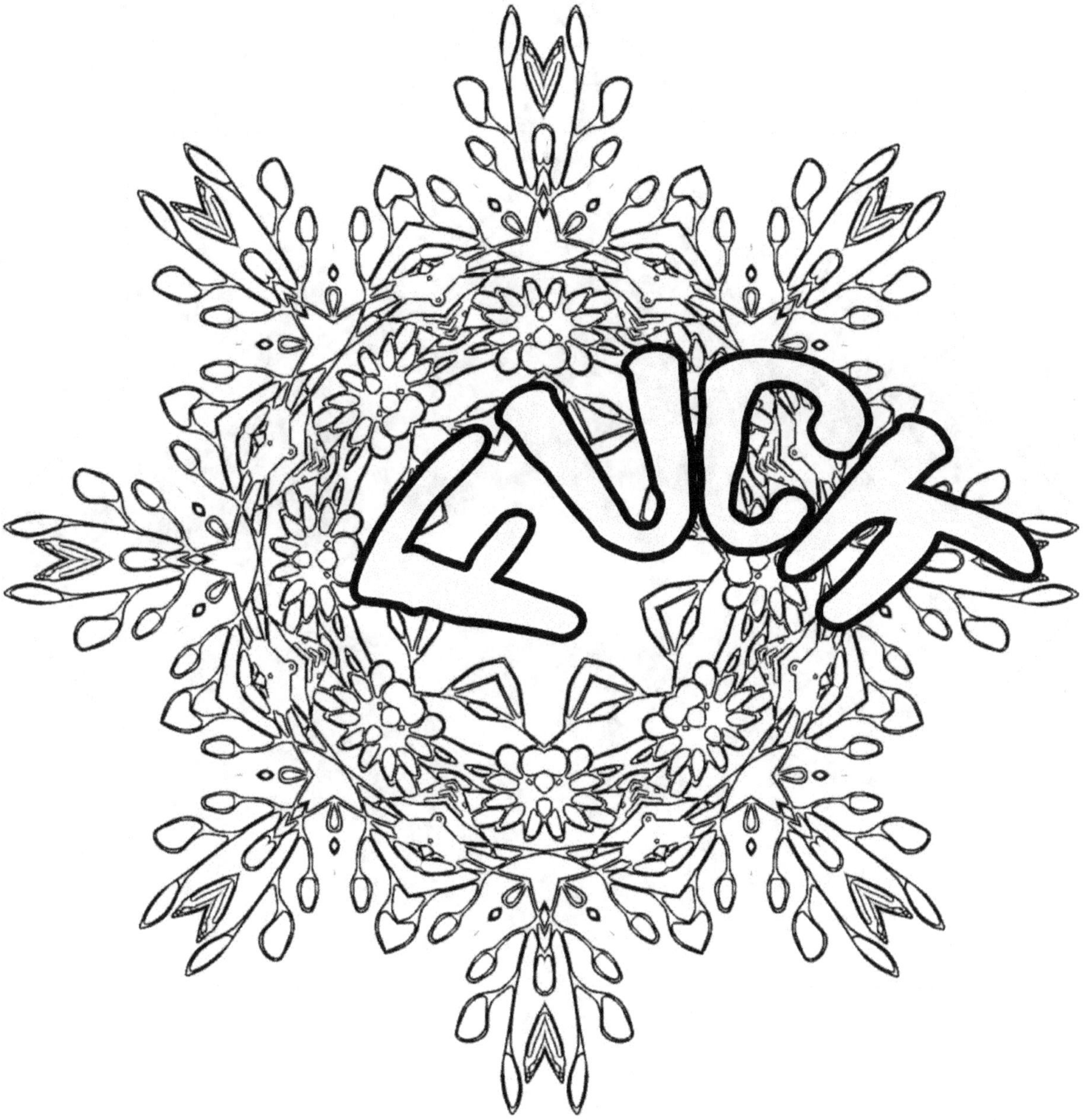
FUCK

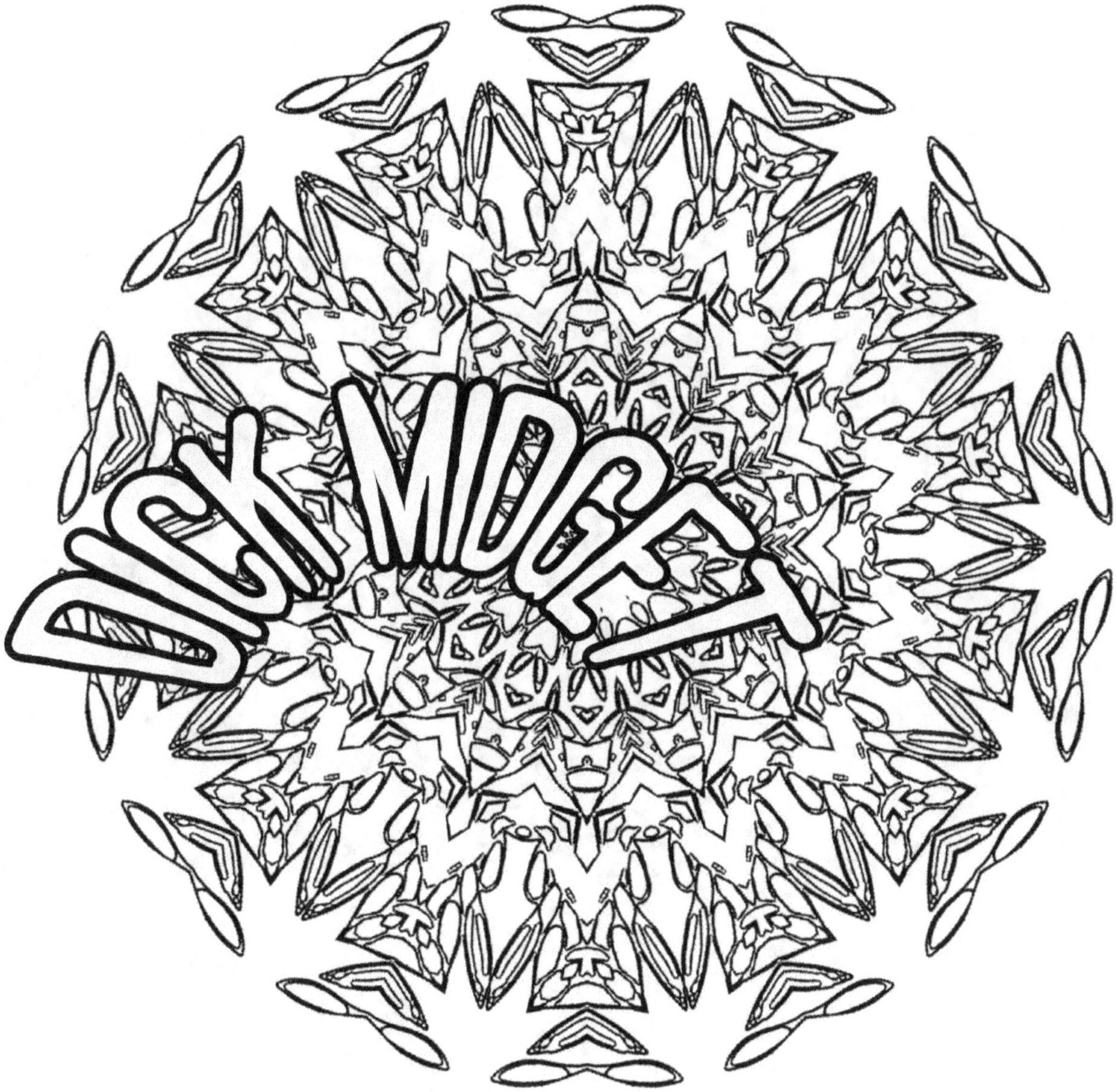
DICK MIDGET

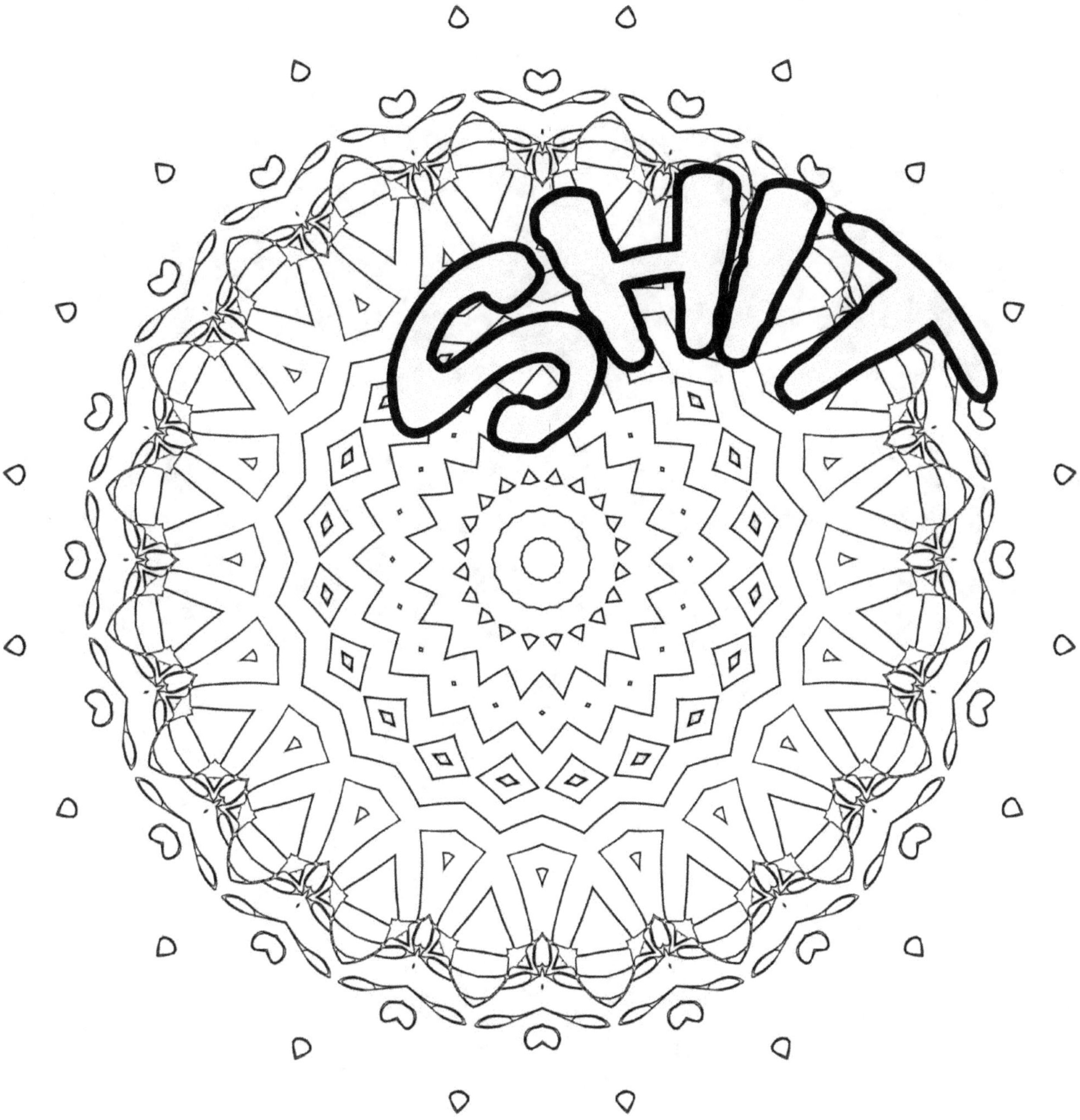
SHIT

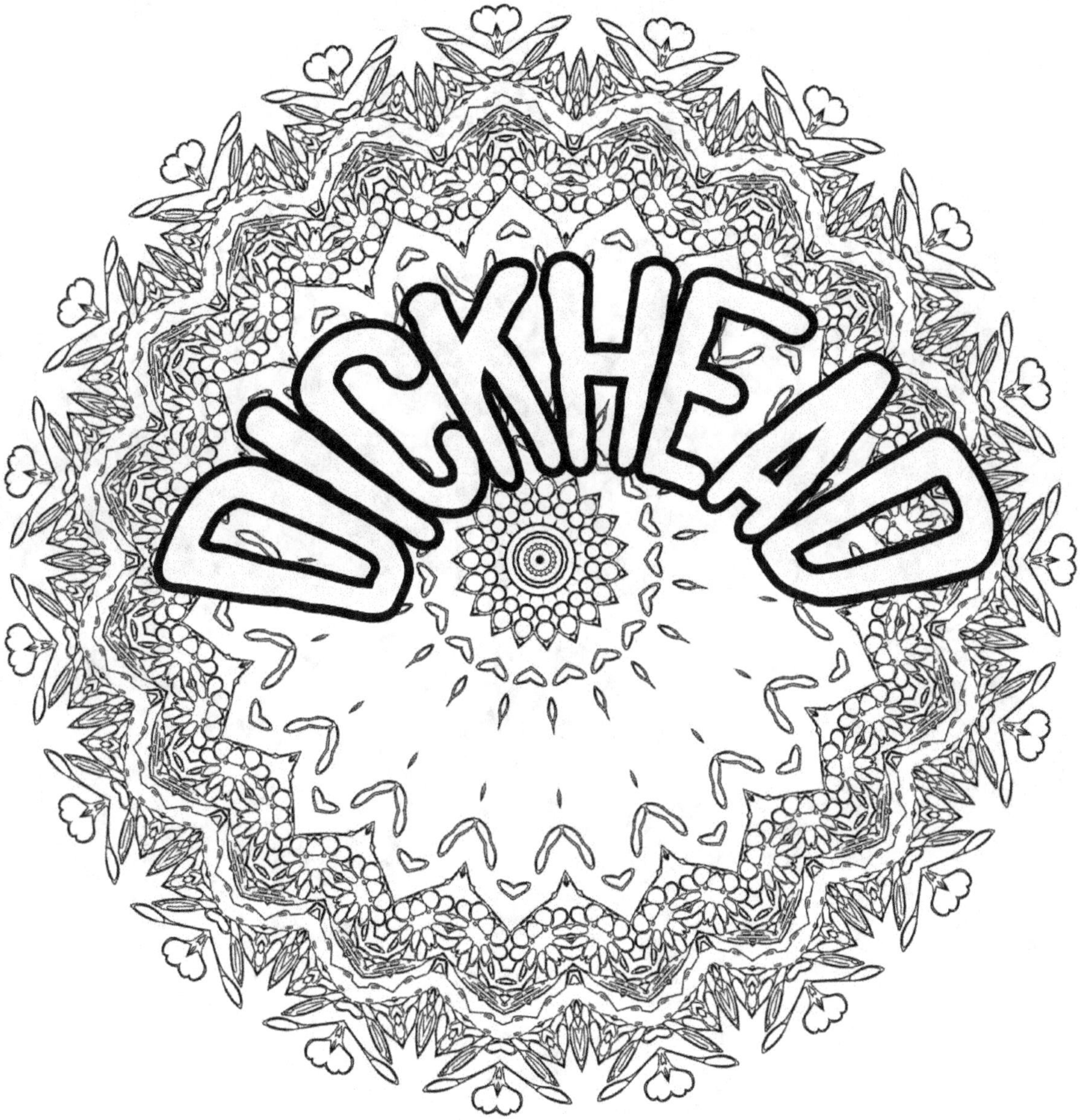
DICKHEAD

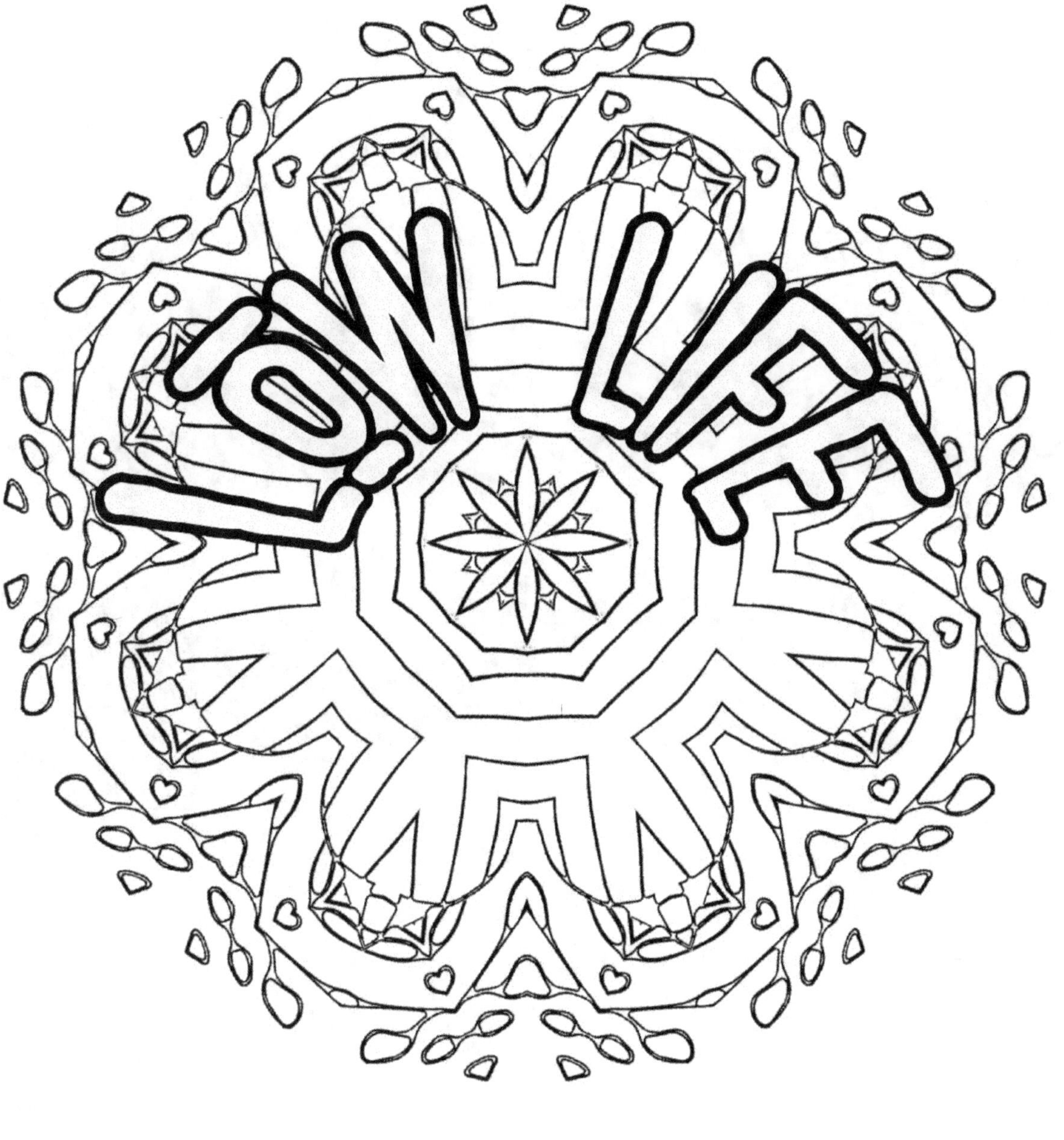
LOW LIFE

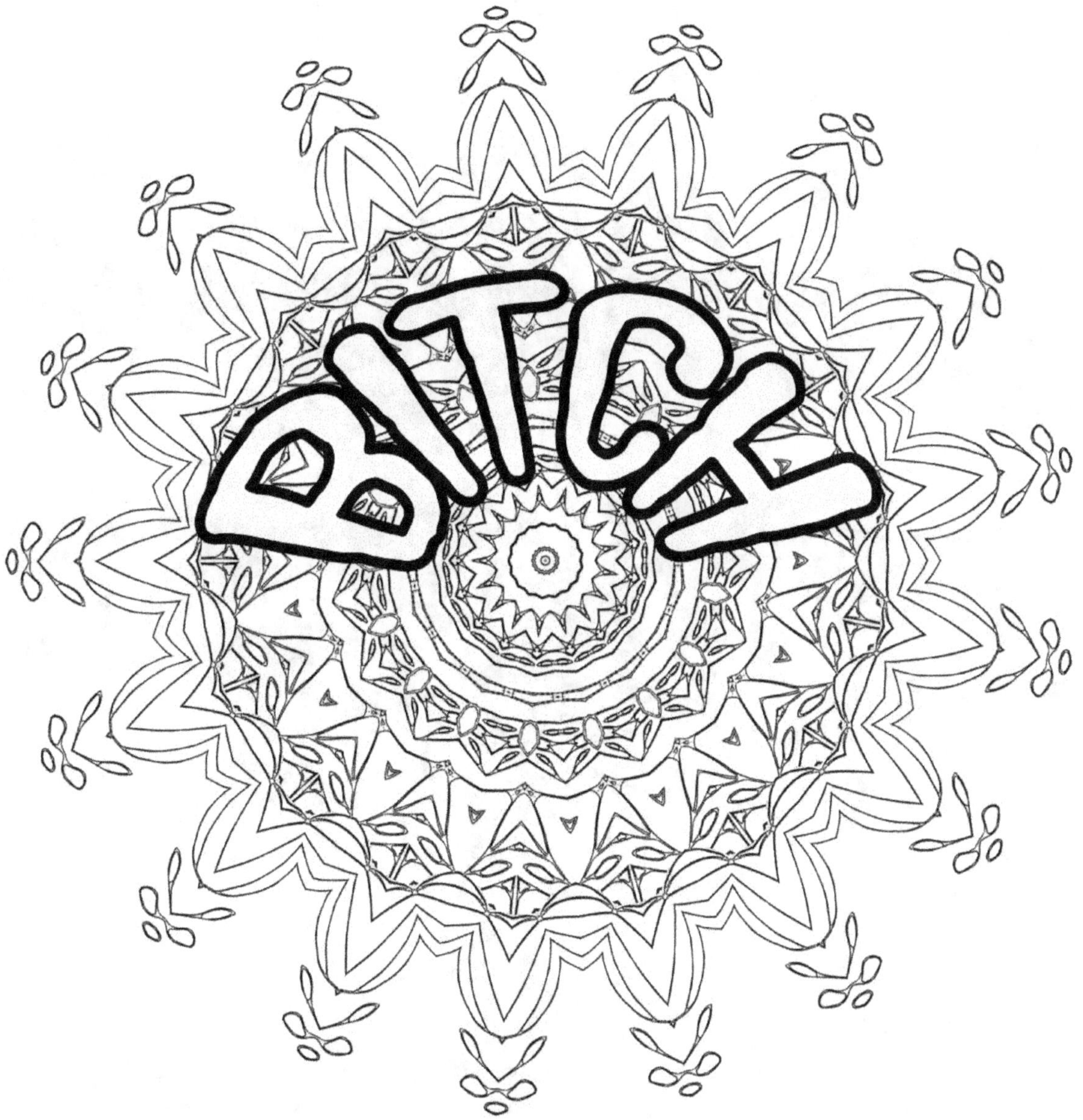
BITCH

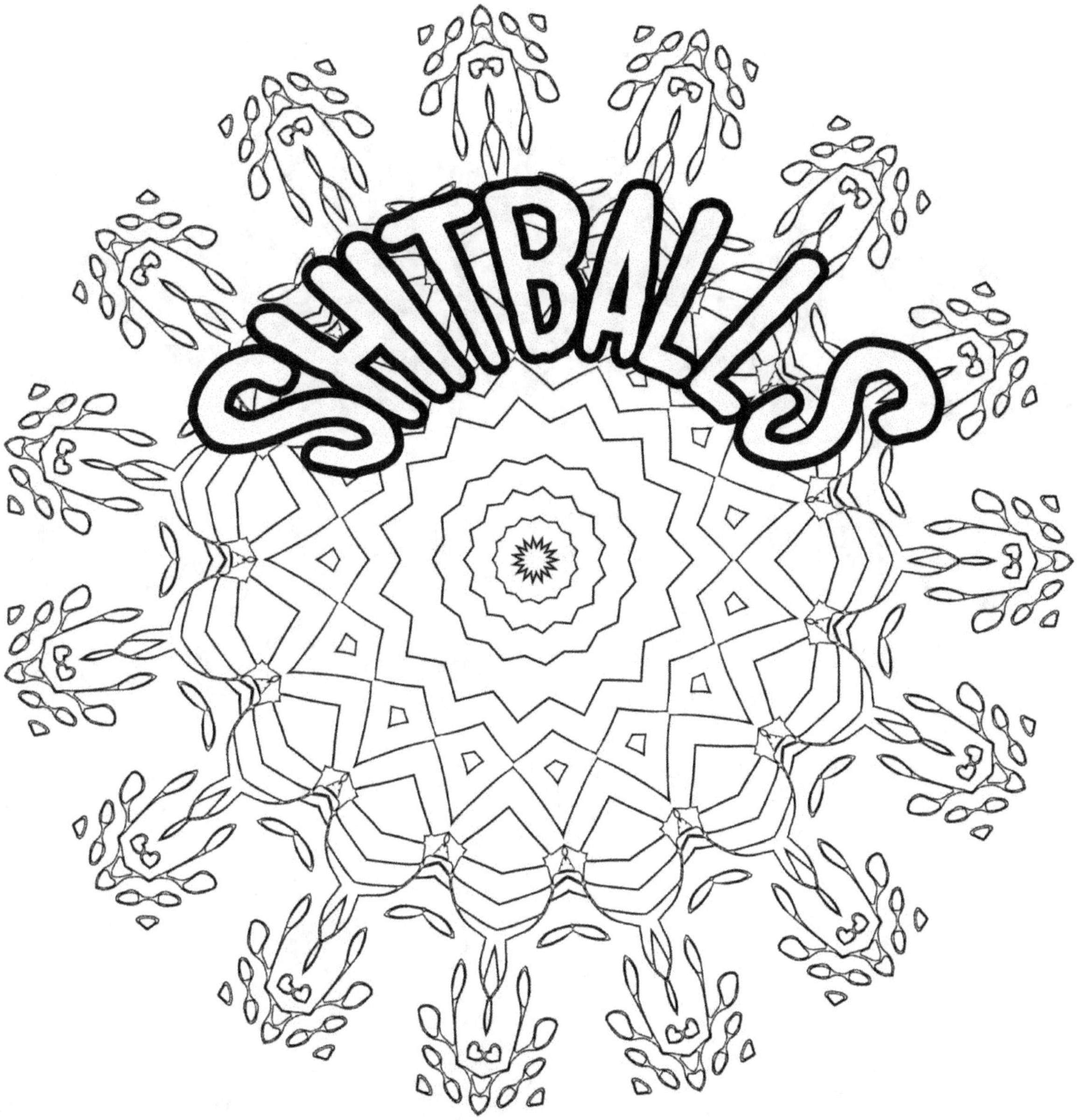
SHITBALLS

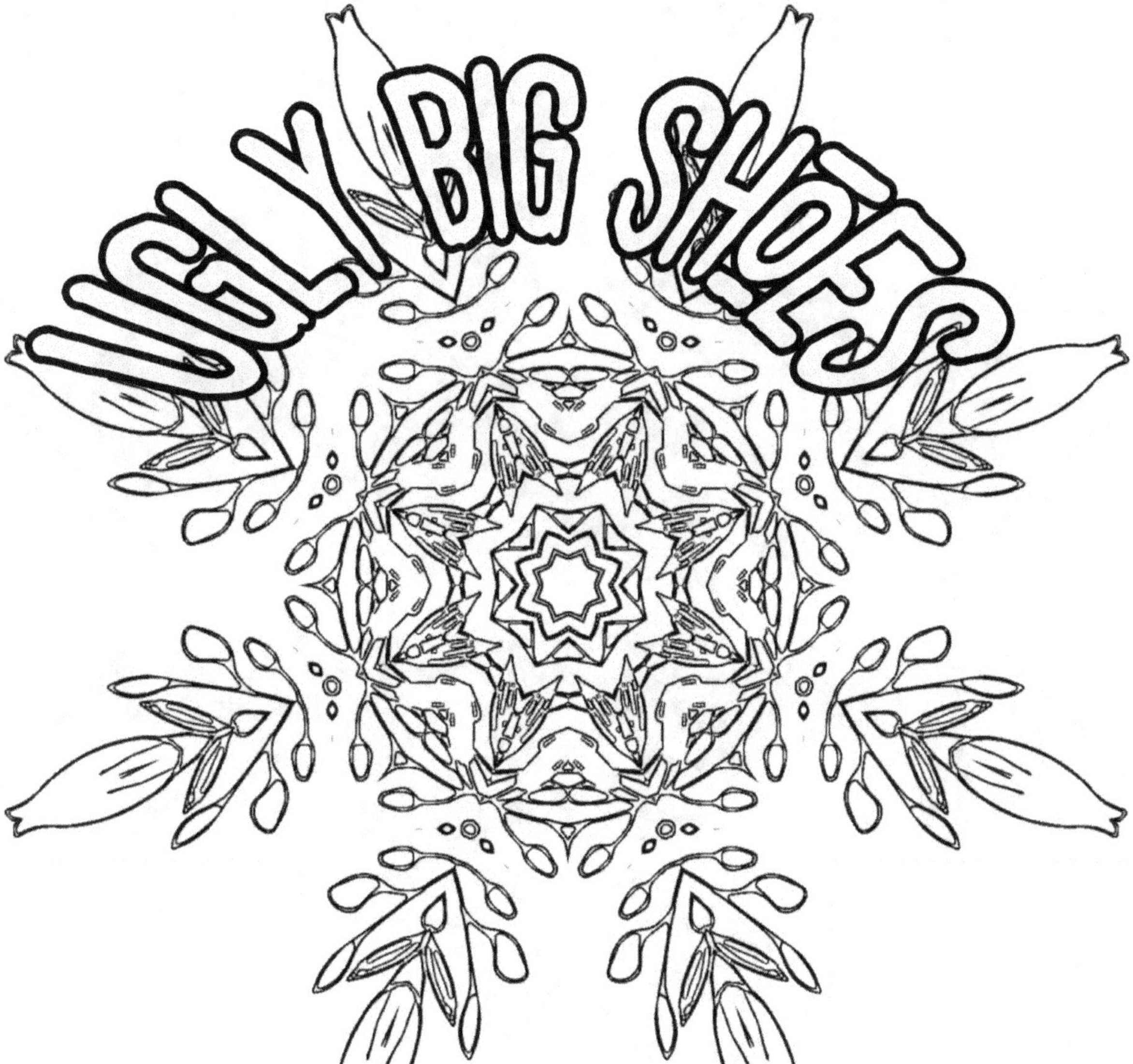
UGLY BIG SHOES

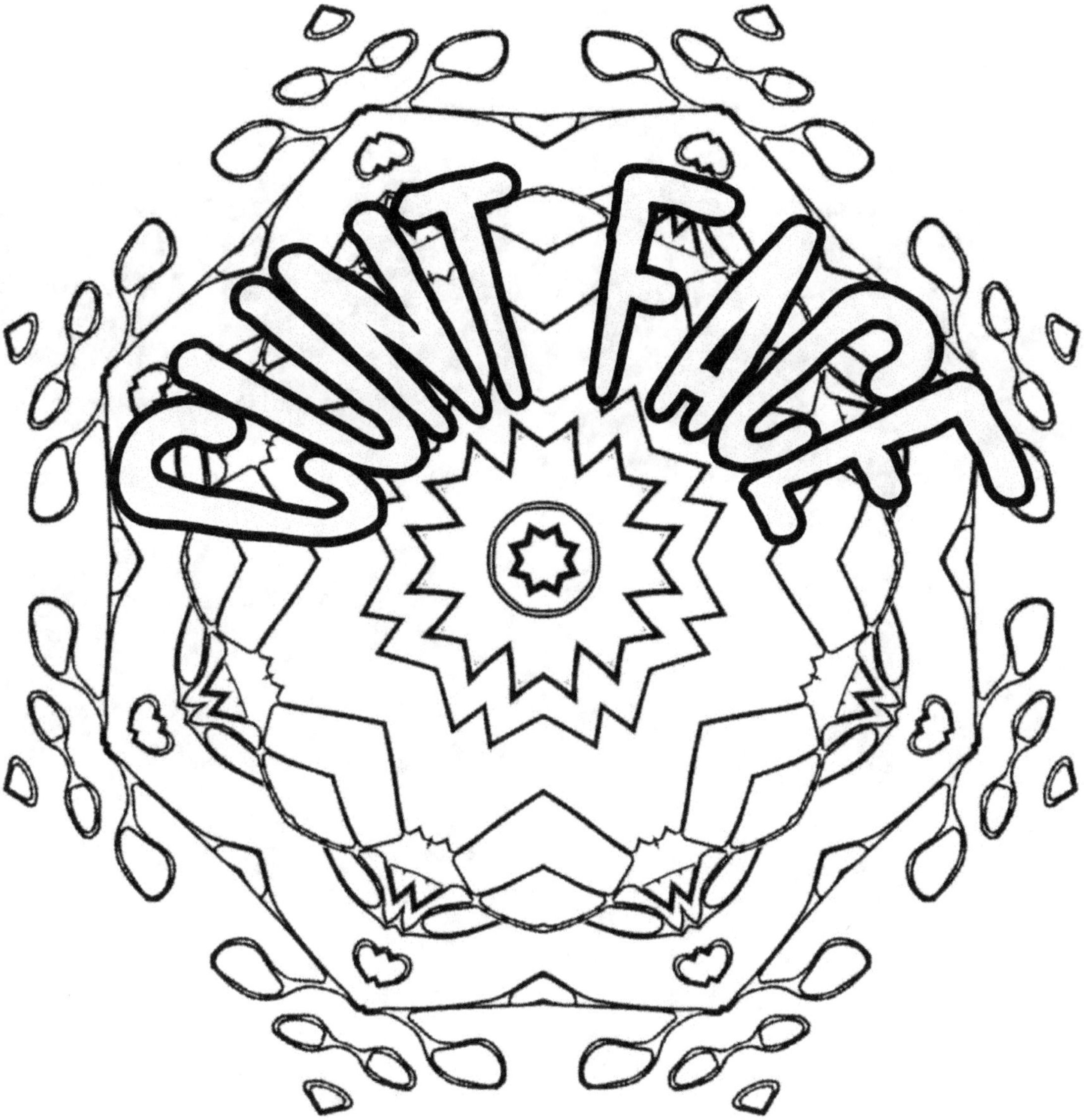
CUNT FACE

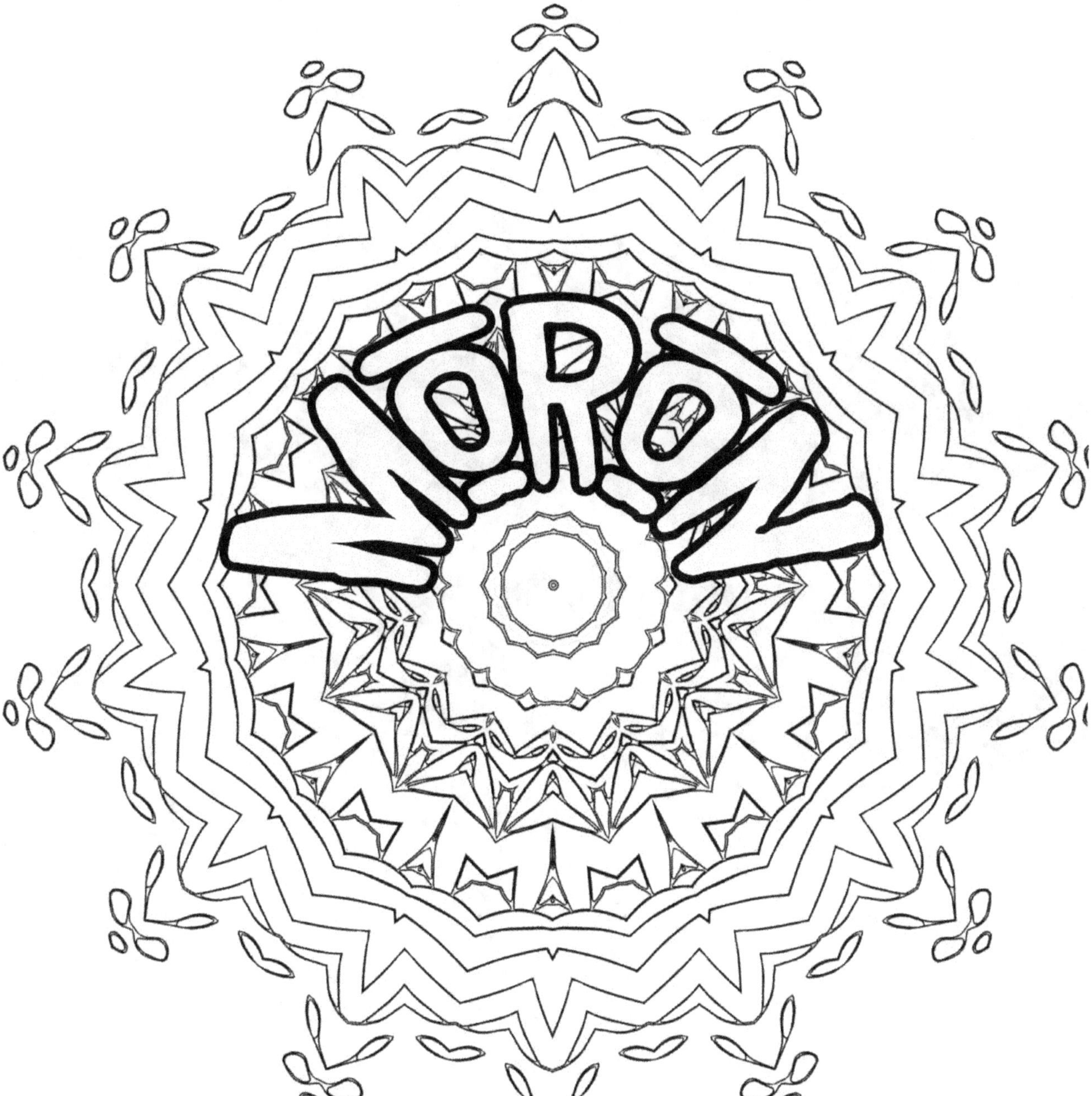
MORON

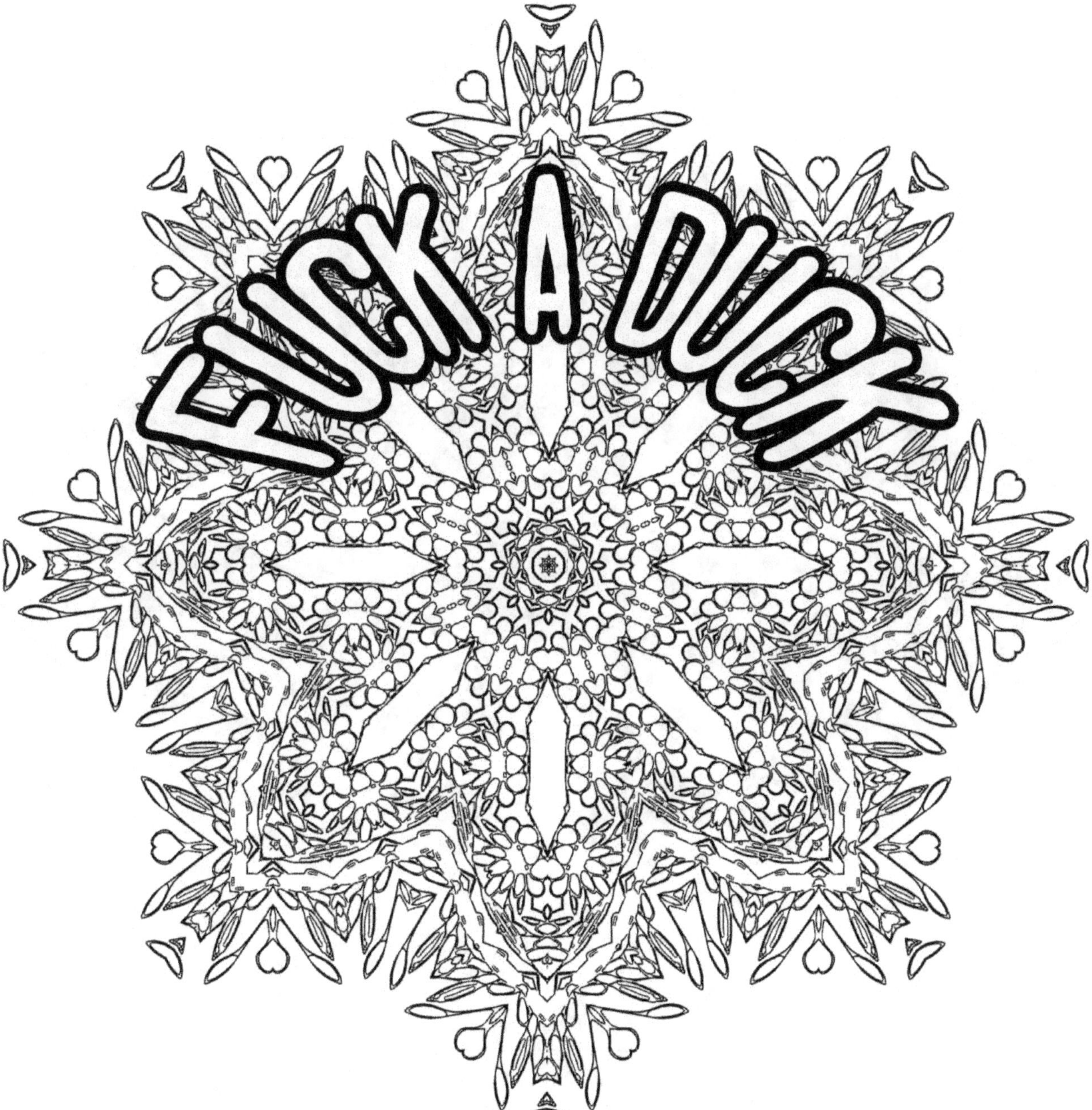
FUCK A DUCK

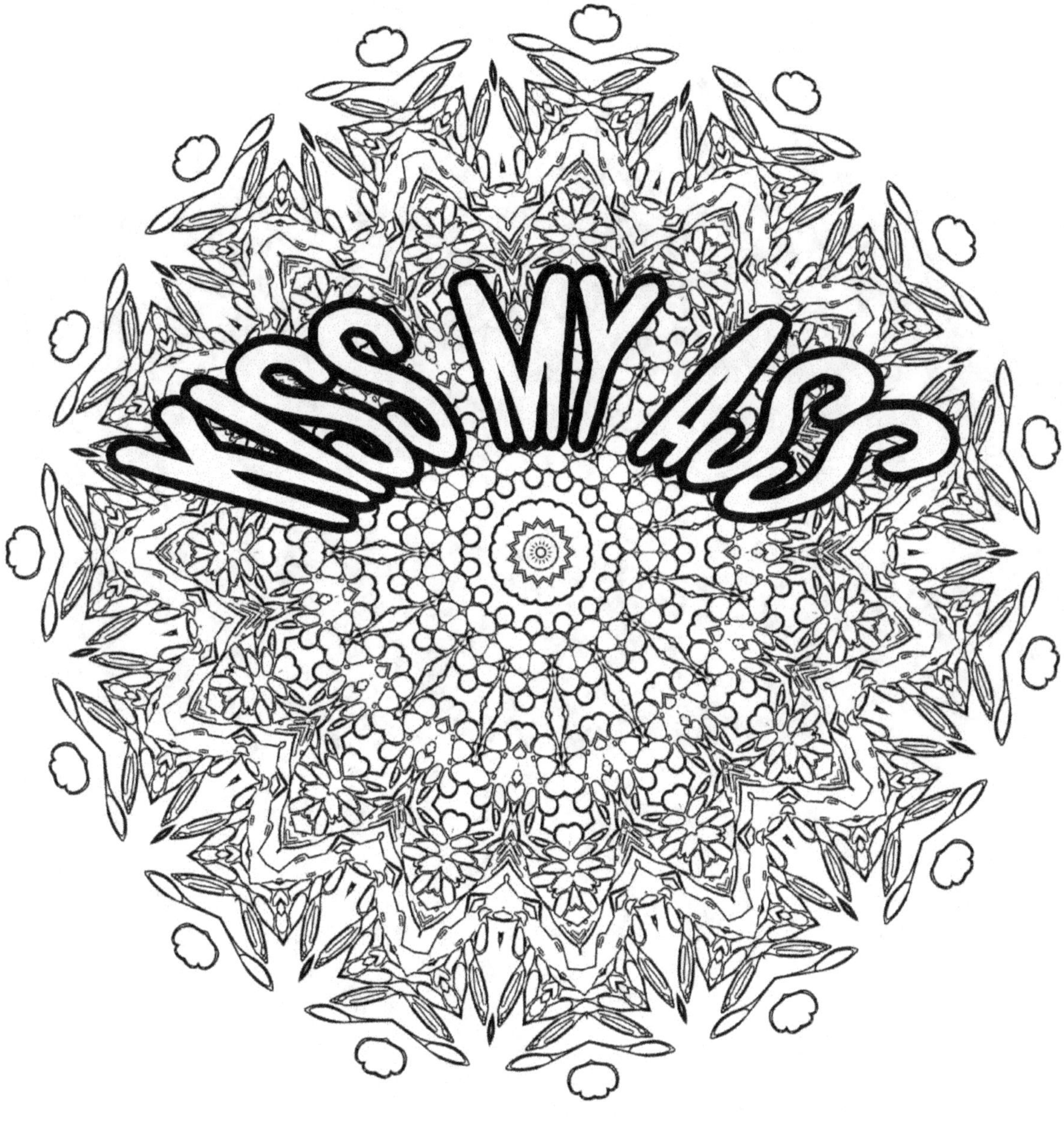
KISS MY ASS

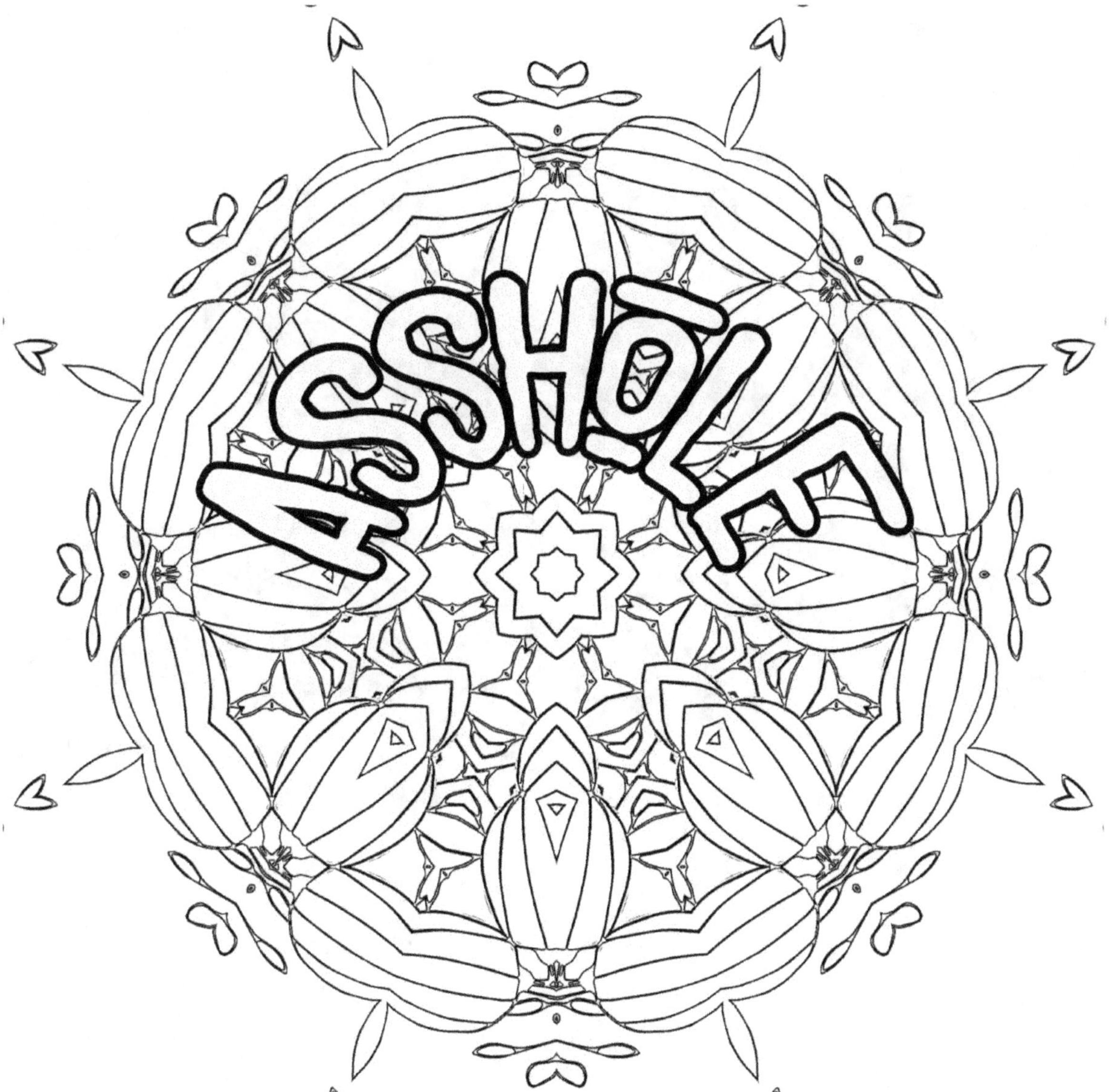
ASSHOLE

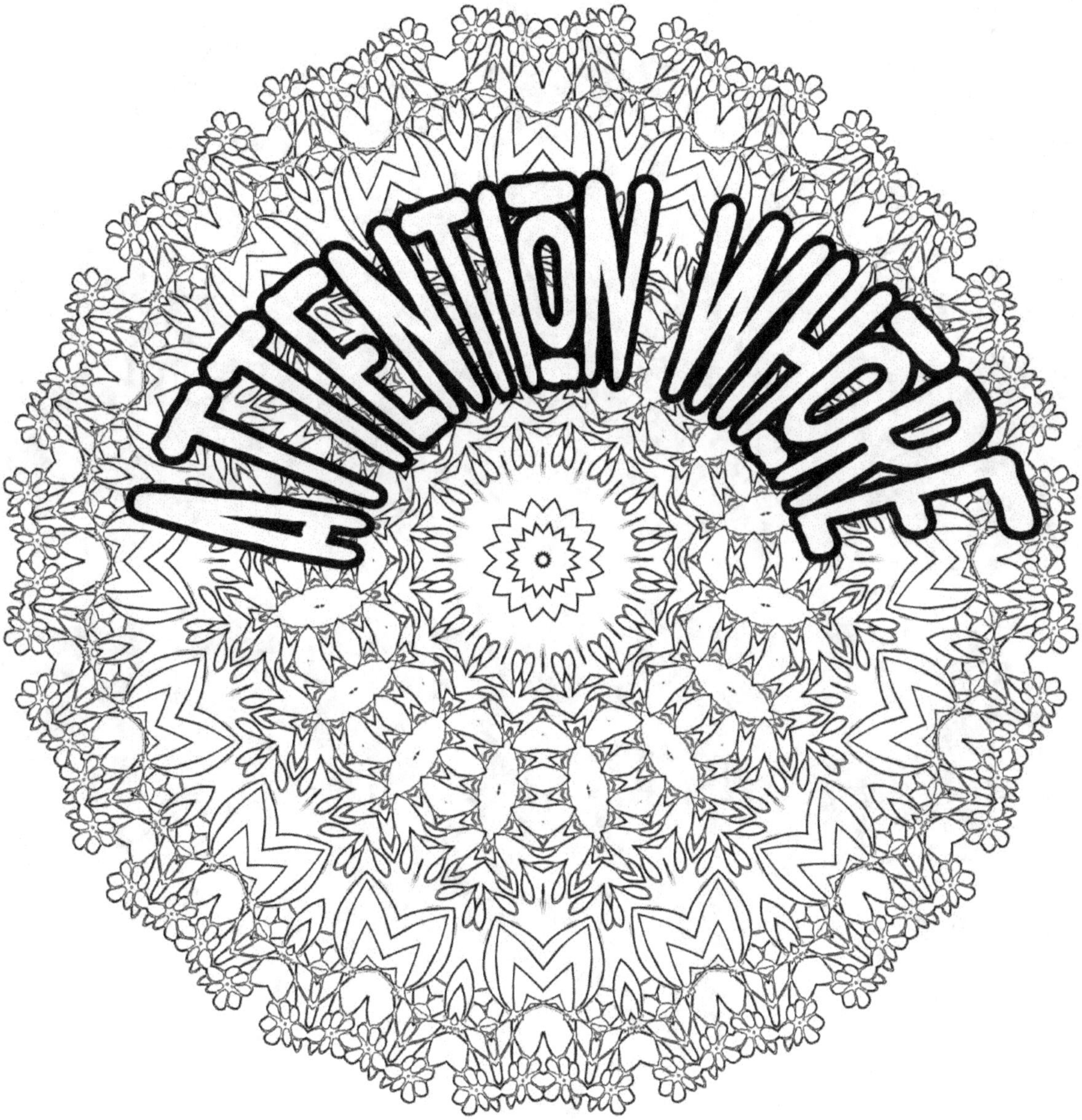
ATTENTION WHORE

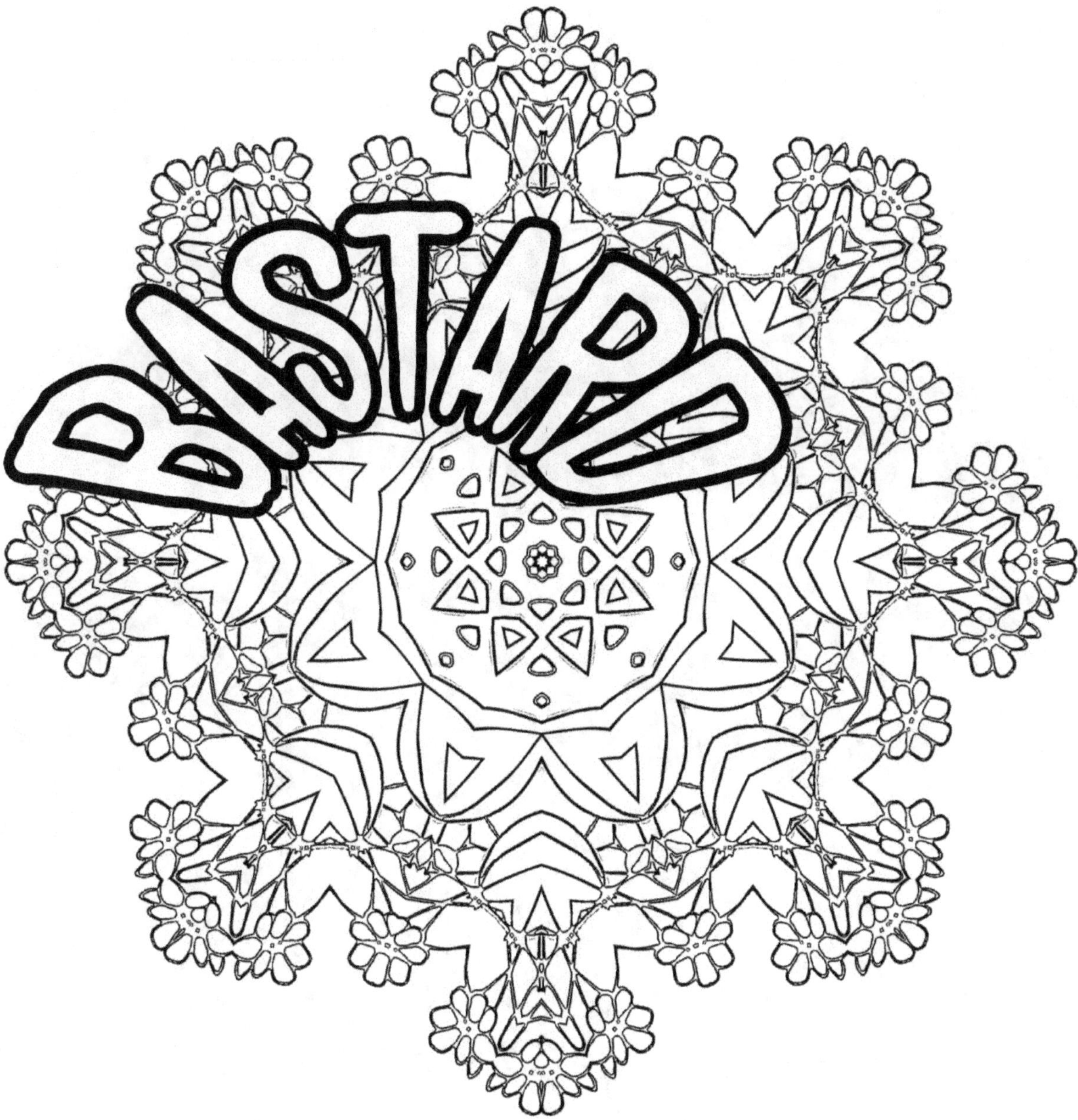
BASTARD

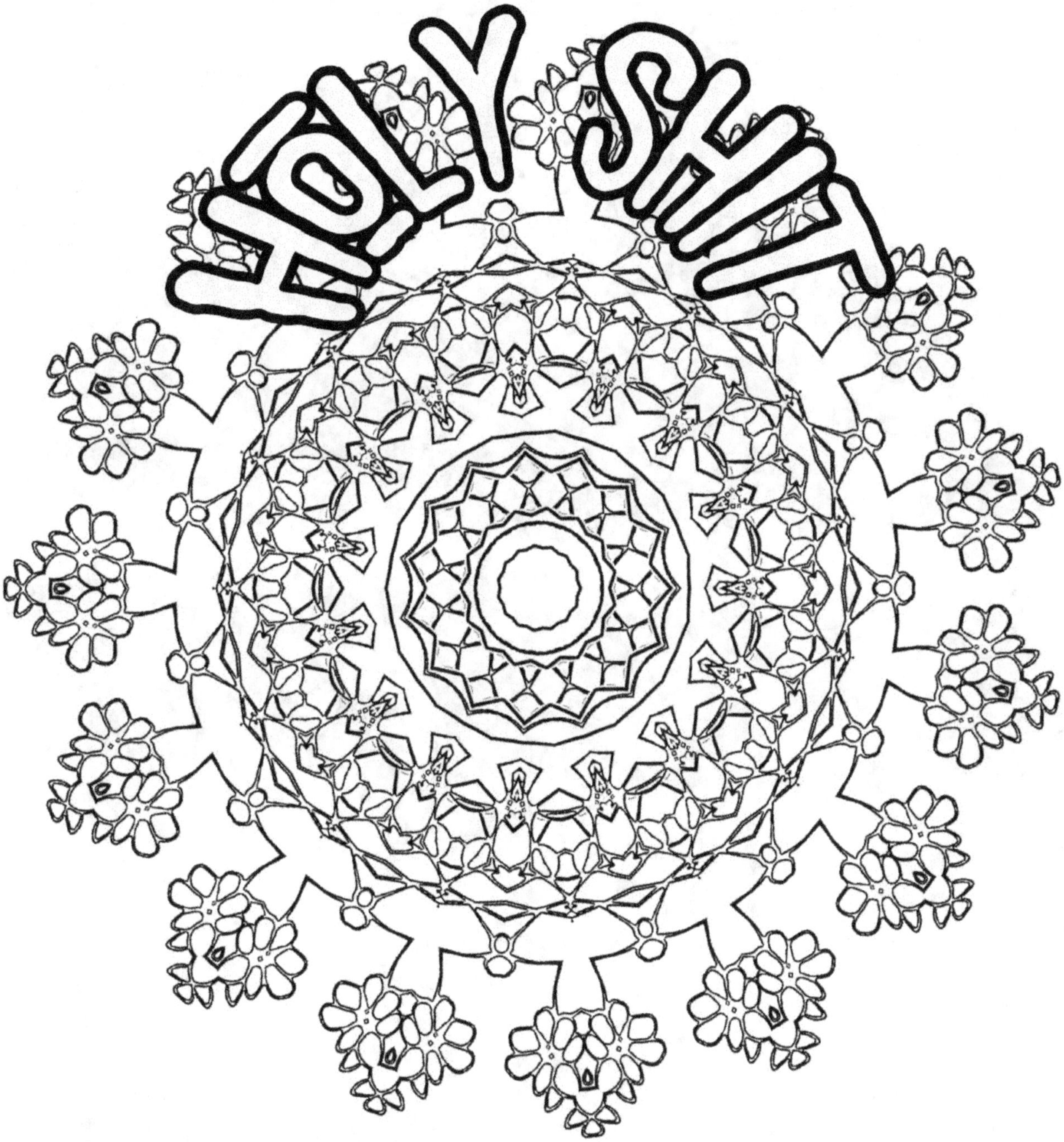
HOLY SHIT

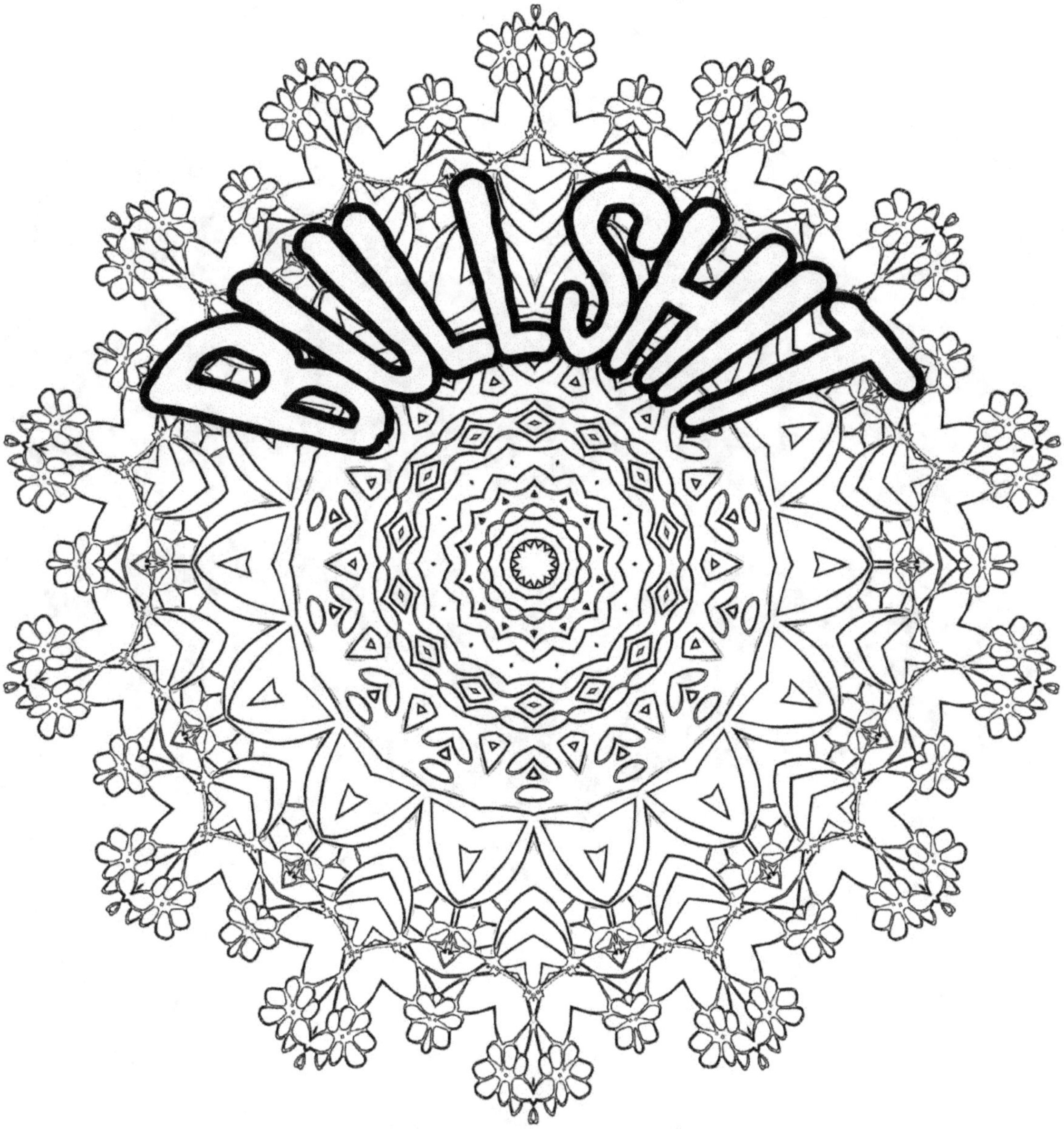
BULLSHIT

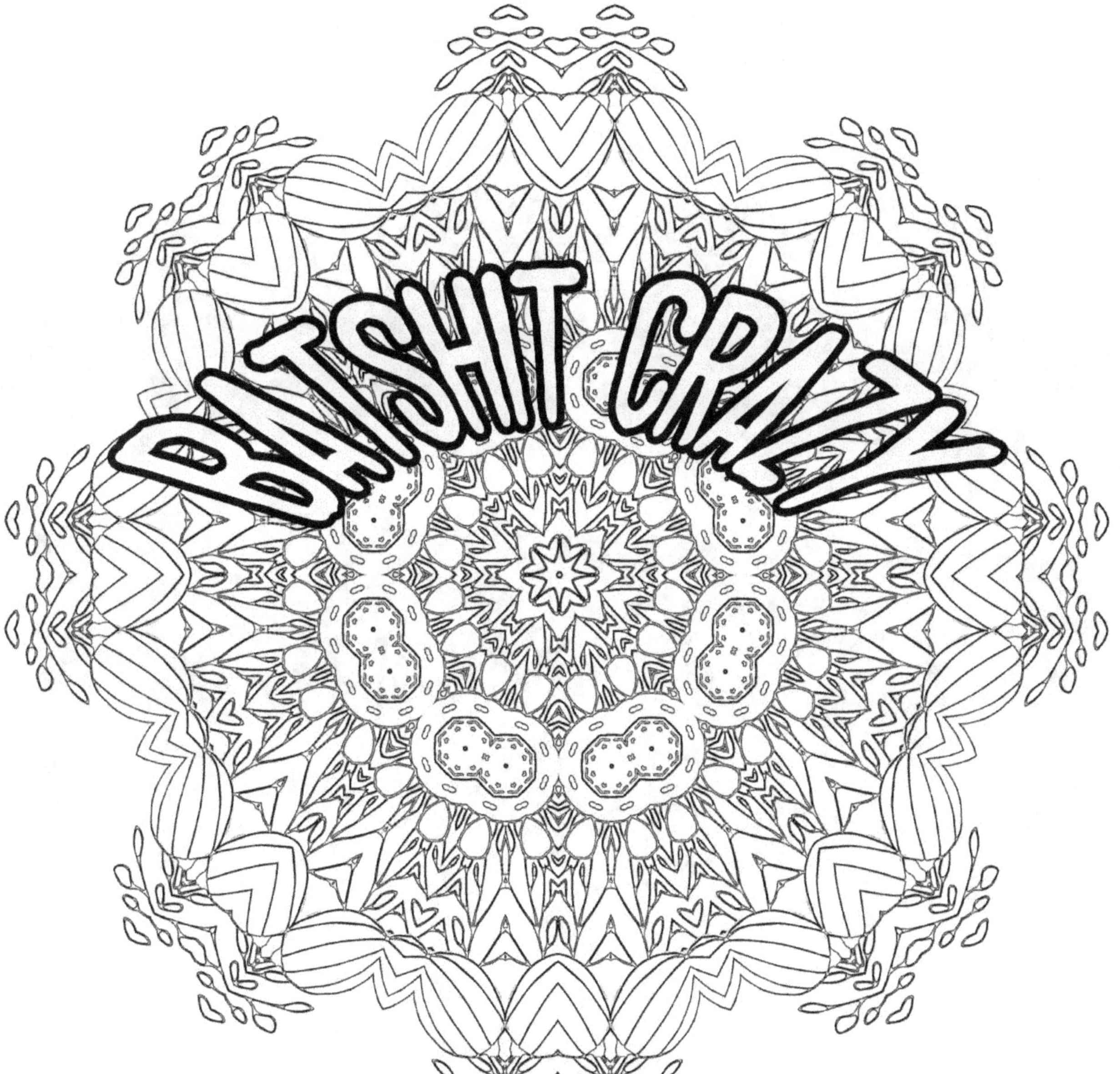
BATSHIT CRAZY

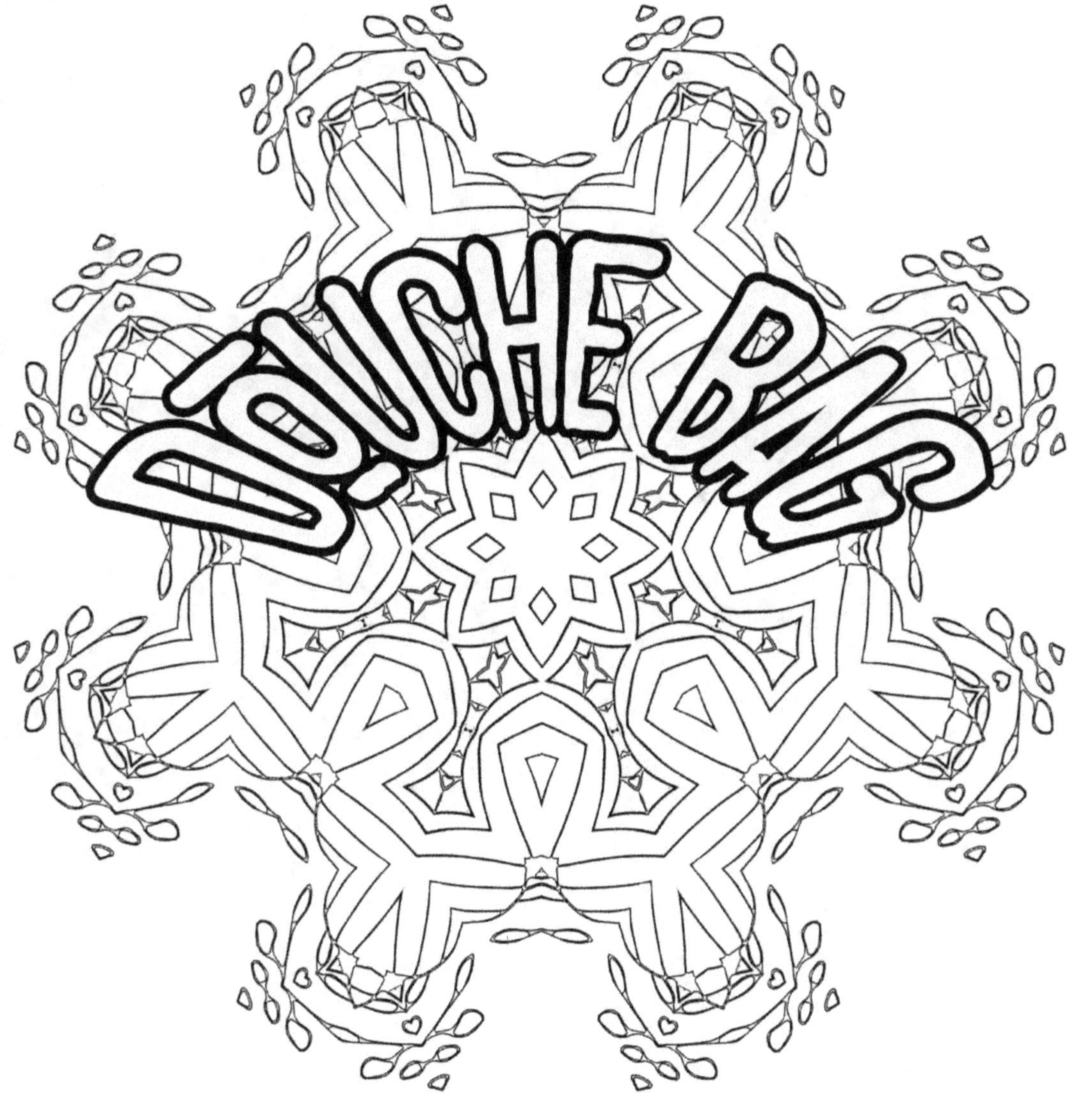
DOUCHE BAG

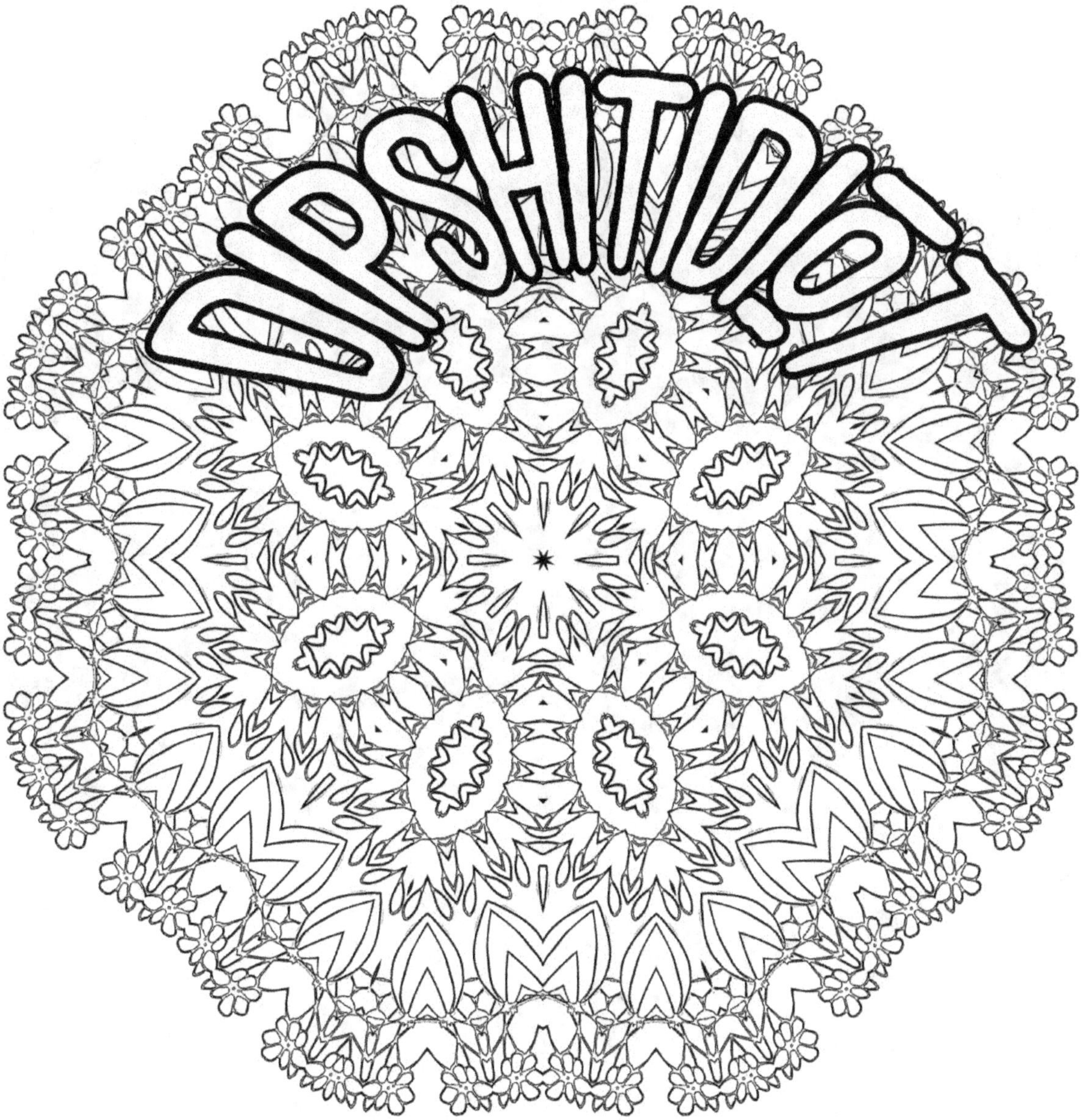
DIPSHITIDIOT

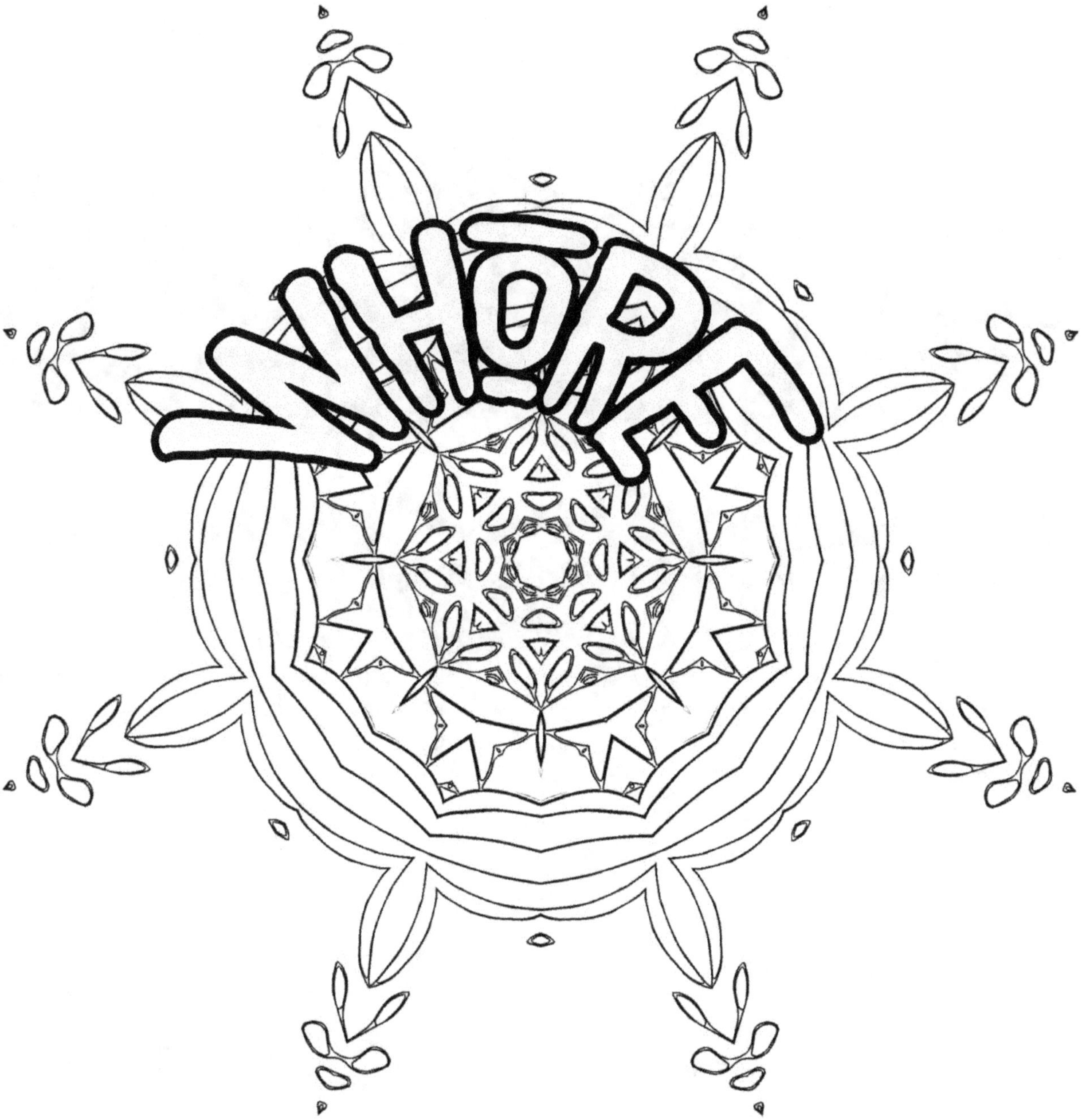
WHORE

www.ingramcontent.com/pod-product-compliance
Lightning Source LLC
Chambersburg PA
CBHW081747170526
45167CB00009B/3950
* 9 7 8 1 5 4 4 1 1 6 2 4 2 *